artworld

What Is
ROMANTICISM?

by Kate Riggs

CREATIVE EDUCATION · CREATIVE PAPERBACKS

Published by Creative Education and Creative Paperbacks
P.O. Box 227, Mankato, Minnesota 56002
Creative Education and Creative Paperbacks are
imprints of The Creative Company
www.thecreativecompany.us

Design and production by Chelsey Luther
Art direction by Rita Marshall
Printed in the United States of America

Photographs by Alamy (Ivy Close Images), The Athenaeum (Pierre
Volaire/schroetterjoseph), The Bridgeman Art Library (Caspar David
Friedrich/Nationalgalerie, Berlin, Germany/Bridgeman Images), Corbis
(Brooklyn Museum, Corbis), Getty Images (Eugene Delacroix, Caspar
David Friedrich, Imagno), National Gallery of Art (Joseph Mallord William
Turner/Widener Collection), Tate Images (Joseph Mallord William Turner),
Wikimedia Creative Commons (Francisco Goya/Colección Real)

Library of Congress Cataloging-in-Publication Data
Riggs, Kate.
What is romanticism? / Kate Riggs.
p. cm. — (Art world)
Summary: With prompting questions and historical background, an early
reader comes face to face with famous works of Romantic art and is
encouraged to identify feelings and consider dreamlike subjects.
Includes bibliographical references and index.
ISBN 978-1-60818-629-7 (hardcover)
ISBN 978-1-62832-227-9 (pbk)
ISBN 978-1-56660-695-0 (eBook)
1. Romanticism in art—Juvenile literature. 2. Painting, European—19th
century—Juvenile literature. I. Title.

ND457.5.R65R54 2016
709'.034209034—dc23   2015008504

CCSS: RI.1.1, 2, 3, 5, 6, 7; RI.2.1, 2, 3, 5, 6, 7; RI.3.1, 3, 5, 7; RF.1.1; RF.2.3, 4;
RF.3.3

First Edition HC
9 8 7 6 5 4 3 2 1
First Edition PBK
9 8 7 6 5 4 3 2 1

Contents

Clouds drift in the sky.

Picturing Feelings

A monster stands near a mountain. If you feel sad, scared, or excited, you may be looking at Romanticism.

Sunset at Sea (1906), by later American Romantic Thomas Moran

5

Keelmen Heaving in Coals by Moonlight (1835), by J. M. W. Turner

Dreamy Quality

Looking at Romantic art is like seeing a dream. Sometimes the dream is scary. Sometimes it is colorful. Other times, you might not know *what* to think about it!

What's a Romance?

Romanticism was a time from the late 1700s to 1850. "Romantic" is a word that has to do with feelings. Romantic art is full of emotion. The stories come alive with feeling.

Moon Rising over the Sea (1822), by Caspar David Friedrich

Through the Fog

Caspar David Friedrich painted *Wanderer above the Sea of Fog* in 1818. Pretend you are the man on top of the rock. How would you feel?

The man in the painting is the artist, Friedrich.

Powerful Colors

Eugene Delacroix painted with strong colors. They showed powerful feelings. The men in *Dante and Virgil in the Underworld* (1822) look scared. Their clothes are bright against the dark sky.

This painting is based on a story by an Italian man named Dante.

Art in Nature

Romantic artists liked to paint nature. John Constable was a landscape painter. He made drawings of *The Hay Wain* (1821) outside. Does the sky look peaceful or stormy to you?

Working outside helped artists see changes in light and shadow.

In ancient Rome, Regulus was an army general who was taken prisoner.

Into the Light

Constable's friend J. M. W. Turner focused on light. The color of the sky draws your eye in his paintings. In *Regulus* (1828–37), the light seems to explode. It reaches out to you.

Romanticism and You

How does a Romantic painting make you feel? Can you think of a story to go along with it? The next time you have a dream, try to draw it!

The Eruption of Vesuvius (1771), by Pierre-Jacques Volaire

Portrait of a Romantic Artist

Francisco de Goya was born in Spain in 1746.
He painted **portraits** of the royal family. Then he
started painting scary monsters like *The Colossus*
(c. 1808). His pictures looked like bad dreams.

Left: *The Colossus*; above: *The Family of Carlos IV* (1800)

Glossary

emotion—a feeling such as happiness, sadness, fearfulness, or excitement

landscape—a picture about the countryside

portraits—paintings of people, usually showing their faces

Read More

Kohl, MaryAnn F., and Kim Solga. *Discovering Great Artists: Hands-on Art for Children in the Styles of the Great Masters*. Bellingham, Wash.: Bright Ring, 1996.

Venezia, Mike. *Eugene Delacroix*. New York: Children's Press, 2003.

Websites

NGAkids Art Zone
http://www.nga.gov/content/ngaweb/education/kids.html
Make your own art, and learn more about Romanticism at the National Gallery of Art.

Sing-along at the Metropolitan Museum of Art
http://www.metmuseum.org/metmedia/kids-zone/start-with -art/sing-along
Sing along to identify paintings by famous artists.

Index